HOW TO BE
TEN TIMES BETTER
THAN YOUR PEERS

How to Be Ten Times Better Than Your Peers

Copyright © 2015 Victor Ansor. All Rights Reserved.

No rights claimed for public domain material, all rights reserved. No parts of this publication may be reproduced, stored in any retrieval system, or transmitted in any form or by any means, electronic, mechanical, recording, or otherwise, without the prior written permission of the author. Violations may be subject to civil or criminal penalties.

Library of Congress Control Number: 2015958833

ISBN: 978-1-63308-197-0 (paperback)
ISBN: 978-1-63308-198-7 (ebook)

Interior Design by R'tor John D. Maghuyop
Cover Illustration by Miša Jovanović

1028 S Bishop Avenue, Dept. 178
Rolla, MO 65401

Printed in the United States of America

HOW TO BE
TEN TIMES
BETTER
THAN YOUR PEERS

Victor Ansor

CHALFANT ECKERT
PUBLISHING

This book is dedicated

*To God Almighty, the giver of wisdom.
To the memory of my Mother Agatha,
Who brought me to Jesus.
And
To all those who prayed while others laughed.
This is the answer to those prayers.*

*He that walketh with
wise men shall be wise; but a
companion of fools shall
be destroyed.*

King Solomon

TABLE OF CONTENTS

Dedication		5
The Mandate		9
Introduction		11
Chapter 1:	The Wisdom of Daniel	15
Chapter 2:	Discover Your Gifting	19
Chapter 3:	Knowledge Is Power	25
Chapter 4:	Seek God	31
Chapter 5:	Start Small	35
Chapter 6:	Be Diligent	39
Chapter 7:	Plan All the Way	43
Chapter 8:	Understand the Times	47
Chapter 9:	Dream Big	51
Chapter 10:	Be Optimistic	55
Chapter 11:	The Power of Focus	59
Chapter 12:	Love What You Do	61
Chapter 13:	Believe in Yourself	65
Chapter 14:	The Joseph Kind of Insight	67
Chapter 15:	Mind Your Friends	71
Chapter 16:	Avoid Time Wasters	79
Chapter 17:	Overcome Peer Pressure	83
Chapter 18:	Stand Out	85
Chapter 19:	Refuse to Compromise	87

Chapter 20:	Get a Mentor	89
Chapter 21:	The Power of Meditation	93
Chapter 22:	Dress to Be Addressed	97
Chapter 23:	Release Your Angels	101
Chapter 24:	Integrity	107
Chapter 25:	An Attitude of Thanksgiving	113
Chapter 26:	Covenant Practice	119
Chapter 27:	Kingdom Service	125
Chapter 28:	Avoid Bitterness	129
Chapter 29:	Be Bold	133
Chapter 30:	Prayer: The Key	137
Epilogue		143

THE MANDATE

Unto me, who am less than the least of all saints, is this grace given, that I should preach among the Gentiles the unsearchable riches of Christ; And to make all men see what is the fellowship of the mystery, which from the beginning of the world hath been hid in God, who created all things by Jesus Christ: To the intent that now unto the principalities and powers in heavenly places might be known by the church the manifold wisdom of God, According to the eternal purpose which he purposed in Christ Jesus our Lord.

EPHESIANS 3:8-11

INTRODUCTION

Success is relative. What you may see as success may not be the same as how another person views it. At the level where you are struggling to make ends meet can be term successful, considering where you started to get to where you are now. Success cannot be measured in terms of money; no matter how much you acquire in life you may not be as successful as someone who has no bank account. Success is defined as where you started and how far you have come, the hurdles you have jumped through to get to where you are today. For example, If you have to manage to put yourself through high school or college while working jobs at the same time and you finally get your high school diploma, or college degree, that could be considered as success. You need not compare yourself to others who might have more money or better things than you have. You are as successful, although perhaps on a different level.

Although success is relative, there are those who are obviously more successful than others. To be more successful than where you are and to reach that peak that you so desire, there are things you must know and am going to show you by the help of the Holy

Spirit, principles that will make you more successful. I take this to be your new year because what you will know now will set you apart and distinguish you. In every new year, people make resolutions and plans to be better or to reach a certain height no matter what their achievements had been in the previous year. So the information you will get here, is vital to your next level no matter where you are in life now.

> *I have more understanding than all my teachers:*
> *for thy testimonies are my meditation.*
> PSALM 119:99

Having more understanding than your teachers have means you are ten times better than your peers, because it is these same teachers who have taught you and your peers. This prove it is possible to be ten times better than your peers.

> *For I will give you a mouth and*
> *wisdom, which all your adversaries*
> *shall not be able to gainsay nor resist.*
> LUKE 21:15

God can give you wisdom that none of your peers can deny or resist. Your own peers will not be able to measure up to you. You will be far better than them and be preferred to them. God wants us to succeed more than you can ever imagine. If you think you already know everything or have reached a level of success such that you don't need more information, you are headed for frustration, because you can never know too much. The greatest enemy of your progress is your last success, according to Myles Munroe. No matter how successful you are, you still need to acquire more information in order to become even more successful. A businessman who doesn't want more information or doesn't want to bother learning more will soon be out of business, because every day new ideas and innovations will come up that will outshine his old ideas. God says in Joshua 1:8:

> *This book of the law shall not depart out of thy mouth; but thou shalt meditate therein day and night, that thou mayest observe to do according to all that is written therein: for then thou shalt make thy way prosperous, and then thou shalt have good success.*

In order to be successful you need to continuously gather relevant information. The Bible verses you read yesterday will not bring the success you need today; you need to meditate on it continually in order to be successful. In the school of success, everyone is a learner; the more you learn, the more successful you become. This is your new year—and with this book you will learn how to be better, how to start all over and be ten times better than your peers no matter where you may find yourself now. Come on board as we take a flight to the world of unending success.

Anchor Scripture

And in all matters of wisdom and understanding, that the king inquired of them, he found them **ten times better than** *all the magicians and astrologers that were in all his realm.*

Daniel 1:20

CHAPTER 1

THE WISDOM OF DANIEL

*Wisdom is the principal thing;
therefore get wisdom: and with all
thy getting get understanding.*
PROVERBS 4:7

To succeed in life, we need wisdom. We certainly cannot excel in our business, career, family life, academics or ministry at a higher level than the wisdom we possess. To be ten times better than your peers, you need the wisdom of Daniel. The scriptures say that he was able to understand things that others could not and that he had an excellent spirit. Because of this excellent spirit and wisdom, Daniel excelled in his political and administrative career in ancient Babylon; in fact, he was preferred to all the magicians and astrologers.

Many people think that they can excel in life just by going to school and acquiring a degree. This is not true; I have seen many graduates who are sweeping floors just to get by because they couldn't get a job. Education is good, but it is true wisdom that distinguishes us. Daniel was so important in the kingdom of Babylon that every king who came into power sought his wisdom. He served in four regimes just on the basis of his wisdom. In our present age, we need to excel in Daniel's kind of wisdom. You cannot be ten times better than your peers without wisdom; you need it to set you apart from your peers. And like Daniel, when they don't have the answers they will have to come to you for your wisdom.

If all you know is what you were taught in school, you are the most ignorant person on the earth. You must know more than what you were taught in school, and there must be a source into which you are tapping. The wisdom of Daniel did not come from the books he read or from his teachers, but from a supernatural source.

> *The Chaldeans answered before the king, and said,* ***There is not a man upon the earth that can shew the king's matter:*** *therefore there is no king, lord, nor ruler, that asked such things at any magician, astrologer, or Chaldean. And it is a rare thing that the*

> *king requireth, and* **there is none other that can shew it before the king, except the gods, whose dwelling is not with flesh.**
> DANIEL 2:10-11

The magicians and men of wisdom at this time told the king that what he was asking of them was not possible with humans, but what they said no human could handle was exactly what Daniel handled without stress. You see, it is this kind of wisdom that can make you ten times better than your peers, because it is the kind of wisdom that is not found on the earth. What the contemporaries of Daniel did not know was that the gods whom they thought were the only answer to their human problems, was the only true God whom Daniel was drawing from. The source of Daniel's wisdom was the God of the heavens; he was the source from which Daniel drew, and he is still the source for anyone who wishes to obtain Daniel's kind of wisdom. To be more successful in life than your peers, you must know more than your peers. But 'you cannot know more just by reading the same books or attending the best educational institution. Daniel was trained by the same teachers who trained his peers, but he connected himself to God and so set himself apart by divine wisdom. God can set you apart, too, by divine wisdom—if you are connected to him. If you want divine wisdom, ask God,

*If any of you lack wisdom, let him ask of God,
that giveth to all men liberally,
and upbraideth not; and it shall be given him.*
JAMES 1:5

The wisdom of Daniel is available through God, and he will give you that wisdom if you ask him. There are many high flyers today who operate solely on the same wisdom God gave to Daniel. The reason why many people cannot go far in life is because they think they can do it on their own simply through the certificates they have been able to acquire. They cannot bring themselves to ask God for wisdom, and some of them end up doing such foolish things that we sometimes wonder if they are educated at all.

*For the Lord giveth wisdom: out of his mouth
cometh knowledge and understanding.*
PROVERBS 2:6

Wisdom comes only from God. He is the source; without him we are exposed only to limited information. With God's wisdom your business, career and family life will function well and you will become the envy of all the people around you. Therefore, seek for Daniel's kind of wisdom—it will set you apart and make you ten times better than your peers.

CHAPTER 2

DISCOVER YOUR GIFTING

To be ten times better than your peers, you must discover what you were born to do. What is your gift? What is your passion? What is that one thing you will be happy doing even if they wake you up from sleep to do it? It is the discovery of your gift that will open the door of greatness for you.

> *A man's gift maketh room for him,*
> *and bringeth him before great men.*
> PROVERBS 18:16

Your gift can make you great. The great people who are making waves in the world today are those who are using their gifts. We celebrate people in sports, music and entertainment every day, yet we don't sit down to imagine how they got there. It is your gift that brings you before great people, and when you are with great people you yourself will eventually become great. As you are on the journey of life, you have to discover that one thing you were born to do. Everyone born into this world has a gift that came with them, yet many die without discovering their gift. When you discover your gift, you have opened the door to the future. When people come to me for counseling about what they should do, the first thing I ask them is "What is your gift or talent?"—and many times they don't know what their gift is. The discovery of your gift is the highway to greatness.

We were not all born to do the same thing; this is why it is not good to copy someone else. Each of us has a very distinct gift that was placed in us when we were born. To discover your gift, you must first ask God to reveal it to you, and then watch yourself and notice the things you do very often without being told to do so. For instance, if you are in the habit of using any available piece of paper at your disposal to draw imaginary things that everyone admires, you may be an artist. And if you develop that, you may become a celebrity. You may love to sing and have a good voice. When you go into the bathroom you spend a great deal of time singing in the shower; your voice may be your gift. Whatever gives you joy when you engage in it may be your gift. It is your gift that will hopefully determine what you should study in school.

Many people prefer to work at a particular job because of financial security, yet they have a very great gift embedded in them. If they had discovered it and worked on it, they would have been great by now. If you want to be ten times better than your peers you must discover your gift, because this is what will bring you to into the limelight quickly. Many great people whom the world is celebrating today actually did not finish high school. Don't get me wrong. I am not advising you to quit school; education is very important. But I am asking you to look within yourself and discover what you were born with and begin to work on it. Do not let anything or anyone stop you until you are celebrated.

When I was younger a friend of mine was in the habit of dismantling every electronic gadget his father bought. This always got him into trouble, and he received many lashes from his father because of this attitude. Then one day his father's radio was broken and he decided to fix it. He dismantled the whole thing. We were both afraid he would never be able to put it back together because there were too many components. To our surprise, he repaired the whole thing, and the radio worked very well. When his father returned home, he was told what my friend did, and the father gave him a serious beating even though he had repaired the radio. What my friend's father did not understand was that the boy had a gift. If that gift had been harnessed, who knows whether that boy might have become the Bill Gates of Africa today.

You see, there are many people with great gifts who are living in poverty simply because of ignorance. I used to play soccer, and even without being trained I played very well. But I was beaten by my parents on so many occasions that when I see a football I run away out of fear of my parents. If I had been encouraged, I might have been a soccer star today. Everyone born into this world has a deposit of greatness, the gift that you were born with. Your primary task to achieve greatness in life is to discover this gift or talent that came with you. But until you do that, you may just be going through life helping others work on their gifts, and very often you are paid a stipend for such help. Many people bury their own talent and go through life helping others build their particular talent. If you walk through this life without discovering and using your gift or talent, you buried it—and you will have to account to God at the end of life, according to Matthew 25:14-30. You are supposed to use your gift, not bury it. Many parents make the error of forcing their children to go to college and study courses that are not in line with their gift, because they want to have that particular profession in their family. Very often these children end up frustrated in life, because that is not what they were born to do. It is your special gift that will make a way for you in life, not your Bachelors, Masters or PhD. Many of the world's richest people even dropped out of school—if that is the case, what made them rich? This is the simple question we ought to ask ourselves every day as we struggle to make a living.

You were not born to look for job; you came with your work right inside of you. It is foolish to be proud of where you work or for whom you work, because that is not what you were born to do. Many people are talented, but they are busy working for someone else. Google, Apple, Walmart and Microsoft were all founded by someone like you who decided to develop their gift. Yet you work for them, boasting that you have a good job. That is a shame. If you sit down and look within yourself, you can come out with something better—a gift that will make people want to do everything just to work for you. Your gift is everything. You cannot become ten times better than your peers if you work for someone else; in fact, the person you work for is far better than you, because he determines how much you are being paid. No matter how rich you are as an employee, you can never be richer than your employer. But if you use your gift this can set you apart; it will make you greater than your peers and those you used to work for.

If you are a pastor, you must discover your gift, because this is what will set you apart in your ministry. You were born with a gift; God called you into ministry, and the gift is still in you. There are pastors who are born poets, and it reflects in their preaching. Others are excellent administrators, and when they leave and another pastor is sent to that same location members complain that things are not running as well as before. That doesn't mean the new pastor is bad or insensitive; no, administration is just not his gift. Many pastors can sing very well; they have a gift in that area, and many times people come to church just to hear them sing. There are pastors who are comedians; because of this many people are attracted to the church because they make people laugh, and when they laugh they will relax and listen. The discovery of your gift is very essential irrespective of who you are. If you want to be ten times better than your peers, then you must discover your gift.

Chapter 3

Knowledge Is Power

Now that you have discovered your gift, it is time to go for knowledge. All you need to succeed in life is information. Even when we go to church, it is so we can get information that will help us to live right and succeed. It is information that moves the world. After you have discovered your gift, it is vital that you go in search of the information on how to develop and use that gift. Some of this information or knowledge is not embedded in books, but in others who have the same gift. Let me show you how. If you discover that your gift is in soccer, the best way to develop yourself is to go where people are playing soccer, join them and begin training, and before you know it your gift will begin to manifest itself.

No matter what your gift may be, you need information to succeed in using it. Therefore, go for knowledge, and find it wherever you can. You cannot grow to a higher level than your knowledge, so it is important to keep acquiring more information no matter your level in life. It is the level of knowledge you have—a product of gaining information—that will make you ten times better than your peers.

> *Till I come, give attendance to **reading**,*
> *to exhortation, to doctrine.*
> 1 TIMOTHY 4:13

Knowledge is power, and you can get this power through reading. Learn to be a reader, because readers are leaders. You should only stop reading when you stop breathing. Make reading books a part of you. I hear that there are believers who read only the Bible and nothing else. They must be the most ignorant of men, because they will never know anything that is happening in the world. A Christian should hold the Bible in one hand and a newspaper in the other so that as you read the Bible you can see in the newspaper that the scripture is being fulfilled.

> *Study to shew thyself approved unto God,*
> *a workman that needeth not to be ashamed,*
> *rightly dividing the word of truth.*
> 2 TIMOTHY 2:15

If you want to excel, you must study. Study from the pages of books both religious and secular. Identify the books that are related to your gift and study them. You cannot dream of becoming the best chef in the world if you are busy reading only romance novels. Many people waste precious time by engaging in gathering information that adds nothing to their future. There is a lot information out there regarding what you want to become in life, so go for it. Go to the library or log onto the internet. No genuine information you gather today will be lost, because when the time comes that information will produce. Seek people who have made it in their field and find out how they succeeded. You may not be able to reach them personally, but you can through books either written by them or about them. I recently saw a movie about a woman who became the President of the United States after the death of the President. Because she was a woman, her party did not want her and did everything to remove her. But she was resolute and very determined to prove them wrong, so she began studying the biographies of former presidents. She ended up becoming the best President. You see, she went for knowledge by reading about others who were there before her.

Sometimes you have to further your education, if you realize that your gift requires it. Sometimes you have to attend seminars to build yourself. Get videos of people who excel in your field and watch them until you begin to produce like them. As a pastor, get the CDs of pastors who have the same calling and are successful. Watch their videos until something rubs off on you. If you go into the ministry and carry the name pastor without the world knowing about you, that is a shame. Why should you be comfortable being an ordinary pastor? The information you have accumulated may need to be upgraded in order for you to attain a certain level in life. No matter what you do, do not stay in one place; try as much as possible to go for knowledge wherever you think you can find it. If you are an athlete, get some sneakers and go for training with people who are in your field.

Information rules the world. And in this computer age we have a great amount of information at our fingertips. We can easily access any information we want in the comfort of our home through the internet that is available on our phones, tablets, iPads and laptops. We cannot afford to be ignorant in this age. Everything you want to know is available on the internet; all you need to do is search. Information regarding your area of interest is just a click away.

The difference between a successful pastor and others who are not successful is information. Successful pastors read lots of book and spend time on the internet gathering relevant information that aligns with the message they are preparing to preach. They go out of their way to relate to their church members and find out what they are struggling with. After gathering all of this information, they are able to present a message that gets straight to the issues their members are faced with. You cannot succeed in ministry if you only pray and read the Bible and nothing more. People go to church to get information, and when God speaks it is information that he gives to man to help him know what to do. Information is everything; the more you acquire, the more knowledge you will have and the more successful you will become.

Chapter 4

Seek God

If you want to be ten times better than your peers, you must seek God. You certainly cannot make it in life on your own; you need God to succeed.

> *And he **sought** God in the days of Zachariah, who had understanding in the visions of God: and as long as he **sought** the Lord, God made him to prosper.*
> 2 Chronicles 26:5

King Uzziah was 16 years old when he was anointed king of Israel. As a young king, he decided to seek God, and the Bible says as long as he continued to seek God, God made him successful. King Uzziah became ten times better than his peers because he sought God. As you read further, you will see that other kings were paying tribute to him. You cannot become great in life if you neglect God. If you think you can make it on your own, you will be heading for frustration. This is why we see those who are supposedly great people committing suicide or ending up in jail and losing everything they had worked for—because they didn't seek God.

Remember, having lots of money in the bank or driving the fanciest car does not make you better than your peers; there are many who have everything, yet they are not successful. True success comes from God and has nothing to do with lots of money in the bank. You are not successful if you are the richest man in the world, yet you have been a patient in most of the hospitals around the world in search of good health. When you seek God, he will make you succeed—and success from God comes with peace, security, long life and divine health, so you won't need a doctor.

When you seek God as you discover your gift or talent, he will guide you in how to become successful with that gift. He will show you things you had never known and connect you with people who will help you to become great. When God wants to bless a man, he always sends a man. When God wants to make you great, he will send someone to you who will help you to achieve greatness; these individuals are called destiny helpers. I have seen people who were nothing—but had a great gift and God connected them with people who helped them, so today the world is celebrating them.

It is only God who can make you great. If you don't realize this, you will go around begging people for help who will only use you and possibly dump you when they are done. But when you seek God, he knows whom to send your way, people who will not take advantage of you but will help you become successful. Seek God by acknowledging that he is the giver of talents. Whatever gift you have comes from him, and you cannot make it without him. When you do this, you have committed him to your affairs and he will help you.

CHAPTER 5

START SMALL

Every great enterprise started in a corner. Bishop David Abioye of Winners Chapel International once said, "You are permitted to think globally, but start locally." This is very true. To start locally means to start small. Whatever gift you have, start from where you are. If you discover that you have a gift for selling things, that you can talk to anyone and sell anything, it means you are a born marketer. You don't have to wait until you graduate from college with a degree in marketing before you begin to manifest your gift. Start from where you are; buy things at a lower price and then go where there is a need for them and begin to sell them there. If you start like that, you will graduate from college without having to look for job, but will already have built your own business.

If you discover that you are a comedian, you don't need to look for a job on Broadway or on the Late Night Show in New York City. All you need is to perform in your local church or community hall whenever they have an event. Gradually people will begin to know you; someone who has watched you once may recommend you to another person who has a big show, and before you know it the rest will be history. I used to organize shows; there were many artists who asked me to allow them perform at no charge in my shows, and I always gave them the opportunity to do so. Most of those artists are stars now, but what they did then was start small where they were, and they are now where they want to be. No matter what your talent may be, start small and don't despise those days of small beginnings (Zechariah 4:10). There are many music stars who used to sing in the choir in their church, and some were selling their music CDs on the street until they hit it big.

> *And the Lord said unto Abram, after that Lot was separated from him, Lift up now thine eyes, and* **look from the place where thou art** *northward, and southward, and eastward, and westward: for all the land which thou seest, to thee will I give it and to thy seed for ever.*
> GENESIS 13:14-15

It is from this place that you are now, that you can see where you are going. Start that business small; don't look for a big shop before you begin. It may require your selling from the trunk of your car before you own that big mall in the city. Every enterprise always starts small. Sometimes your office will have to be your laptop and your bed at home, and that is where you will put all the ideas together until the world begins to celebrate you. Your fashion designer dream could be a sewing machine in your one room, where you sew only for your friends who may not even pay you. But if you keep at it, international models may be showcasing your design at the New York fashion week. To be global you have to start local. That is what God himself was telling Abraham to do. Start small and you will end big—and not just big, but ten times better than your peers.

CHAPTER 6

BE DILIGENT

Diligence is pivotal to success in life. No one will ever run with your dream for you; you have to sit down and do your own work. The word "diligent" means showing care in your work. Making a constant effort to accomplish something, being attentive, persistent and painstaking—this is what you are supposed to do. It means hard work and being thorough. You certainly cannot be casual about your work and expect to be successful; never mind the talk of becoming ten times better than your peers. The Bible, in Proverbs 22:29, says,

> *Seest thou a man diligent in his business?*
> *he shall stand before kings; he shall not*
> *stand before mean men.*

Diligence can take you to high places in life. There are many people with great potential, yet they cannot work hard enough to get to where they ought to be. Success is sweet, but the price carries a bitter taste—and if you allow the bitter taste to get in your way, you may not become successful. If you want to be distinguished in life, you've got to give it all you have. No student just wishes to pass the exam; they spend countless hours in the discipline of study to pass the exam and get to the next level. Your gift will be useless if you don't work hard to develop it. To enter the circle of great men, you have to work hard to get there. If you really want to succeed, you must pay full attention to your work and not give in to laziness. Hard word does not kill, and nothing good comes cheap.

> *He becometh poor that dealeth with a slack hand: but the hand of the diligent maketh rich.*
> PROVERBS 10:4

If you want to succeed you must work hard. The Bible says the hand of the diligent makes them rich. If you work hard you will become rich in your field. To be diligent, you must discipline yourself. You must discipline your sleep and some pleasures. You can only begin to have fun after you have done what you were supposed to do—"business before pleasure." You have to experience a level of discomfort if you are to attain great height in life. Those who were always studying in high school are now more successful than those who were partying. It is lack of diligence that makes some people go for fast money, and their end is not always good.

Those who win in the Olympics were not sleeping and then just woke up and got a medal, and neither did the world heavyweight boxing champion get the title after sitting down for hours in front of the television. They worked hard to get the title. Whatever you have found as your calling, give everything to it so that you can get what you want. Hard work pays even though it may not be palatable at the beginning. If you want to wait for the perfect time before you write that book, that time may never come. This may mean sitting up a few hours into the night after a hard day at work or school if you really want to become an author. Hard work is like sowing a seed; there is no way you will not reap, because anything you put into the soil must and will grow. Diligence is the highway to success.

CHAPTER 7

PLAN ALL THE WAY

There is a saying, "If you fail to plan, you are planning to fail." This is very true, because planning is very crucial in ascending the ladder of success. Learn to plan all the way. Learn to put words on paper concerning your goals. Sit down and write out the things that you want to do and how you want to do them. Anything you don't write down is lost.

> *For which of you, intending to build a tower, sitteth not down first, and counteth the cost, whether he have sufficient to finish it? Lest haply, after he had laid the foundation, and is not able to finish it, all that behold it begin to mock him.*
>
> LUKE 14:28-29

In the above passage, we see Jesus talk about planning. He says you have to sit down first and count the cost for the project that you have at hand. Most of the time, the things you put down on paper tend to happen exactly as they were written. Before you begin anything, you need to sit down first and plan on how to go about it. Planning is very important because it helps us manage our time well and also shows us the steps to take in achieving our goals. Planning helps us to know where we are and where we want to be. It helps us even in prayers, because you will always pray according to what you planned. For example, if you want to rent a shop to start a business, you will plan on how much you have to pay for the shop. You will write out the things you want to put in that shop and how you will get the money for them. This will help you to know the cost of opening the shop and how much you have at hand. Even your faith will not work if you don't plan. Without planning you will be working on assumptions, and no one succeeds on assumptions. Jesus said we should sit down and count the cost, so we need to compare information and know in full detail what we want and how we want to get it. Half of the job is already done when we plan, because we see clearly the details of our goals and then begin to work in actualizing them.

Planning also helps you to set directions and priorities. You will definitely know where you are going when you plan, and you will also set your targets in the order of their importance. Planning helps you to avoid error and waste; it helps you to know what to do each step of the way. Bishop David Oyedepo said, "If you don't know where you are going, everywhere will look like it." Planning helps you to know where you are going. If you don't plan at every point in your life, you will think you have arrived when actually you have not started. You must remember that if you fail to plan, you are planning to fail.

CHAPTER 8

UNDERSTAND THE TIMES

To be ten times better than your peers, you need to understand the times that you are in. If you do the right thing at the wrong time, it makes it all equally wrong. Even God is a God of time and season. The Bible says in Ecclesiastes 3:1,

> *To every thing there is a season, and*
> *a time to every purpose under the heaven.*

There is a time for everything. To succeed in life you must understand what works at the right time. There is a time to plan, and there is a time to execute that which you planned. There is a waiting period when you do mental preparation for the things you are about to do. You cannot begin to look for a job when you have not obtained an education. The proper thing to do first is to seek the education, and then start looking for a job after you have completed your education. This means that there is a time for education and there is a time for getting a job.

In every time there are certain ways to do things. You cannot bring in ideas from the '70s and expect them to work in this present time. Even God our father has a way of approaching issues, and man, depending on the dispensation he finds them.

> *God, who at sundry times and in divers manners spake in time past unto the fathers by the prophets, Hath in these last days spoken unto us by his son, whom he hath appointed heir of all things, by whom also he made the worlds.*
> HEBREWS 1:1-2

In time past, God spoke to the fathers himself and then through the prophets. After that he spoke to the people by his son Jesus, who came and lived on the earth. After Jesus had gone, God decided to speak to us in this present age by the Holy Spirit. If God decided to bring Elijah and Moses to us now I don't think anyone would listen to them, because their time had passed. God knows how to approach people according to the period they lived in, and likewise we must know what to do depending on the times in which we are living. If you live in America but decide to use the African mentality in operating your business it will not work, because they are different locations with different laws and orientation. As you set out to pursue your dreams, business and career, you must understand how things work.

There was a group of people whom the Bible records as having the understanding of time, and it is one of my favorite passages.

> *And of the children of Issachar, which were men that had understanding of the times, to know what Israel ought to do; the heads of them were two hundred; and all their brethren were at their commandment.*
> 1 CHRONICLES 12:32

The children of Issachar were men who had understanding of the times, and because of this they were in charge of others. Understanding the times will always put you in command and make you ten times better than others. There were only 200 men from the tribe of Issachar, but they were the men who knew what the whole country of Israel should be doing at that time. This means that they were always consulted before any decision was taken. Only 200 men led the entire nation because of their understanding of time.

This is the age of information technology; the world has become a global village. You can stay in the comfort of your home and transact business or communicate with anyone anywhere in the world. Therefore, get to know how things work in your community or country, and you will succeed. Most businesses today don't have shops you can walk into, but are making billions of dollars because they understand the time they are in and have decided to fashion their business to suit the time. Many people now, especially in the city, don't have the time to cook in their houses. They certainly cannot go hungry, because hunger reduces productivity. So some people sat down and thought about this and decided to provide fast food on the go with home and office delivery and drive-throughs. Some artists were discovered on the internet through YouTube. They knew that no record label would sign them and, with their understanding of the times, they decided to record themselves and put it in the internet. They knew that record companies go on the internet to fish for fresh talent, so they were discovered and now are celebrities. Whatever you set out to do, if you understand the times and decide to give it the approach required you will become successful, no matter how long it takes.

CHAPTER 9

DREAM BIG

This world is the dreamer's world. If you dream big you will become big. Don't let big dreams scare you; in fact, if your dream is not big enough that it scares you then it is not worth pursuing. Whatever your talent or gift, dream big, see yourself at the top. It is the size of your dream that determines the size of your future. Dreaming big will change your attitude. No matter how low you may be, when you can see yourself doing big things you will certainly carry yourself well. It is the dream that creates the future. Every great enterprise on the earth today started with a dream, and a man without a dream is a man without a future. Most people don't have dreams; they do not realize that you cannot arrive at a future if you don't see it, and the only way you can see the future is through dreams. Your dream is your vision of tomorrow.

> *And Joseph dreamed a dream, and he told it his brethren: and they hated him yet the more. And he dreamed yet another dream, and told it his brethren, and said Behold, I have dreamed a dream more; and, behold, the sun and the moon and the eleven stars made obeisance to me. And he told it to his father, and to his brethren: and his father rebuked him, and said unto him, What is this dream that you have dreamed? Shall I and thy mother and thy brethren indeed come to bow down ourselves to thee to the earth? And his brethren envied him; but his father observed the saying.*
> GENESIS 37:5 AND 9-11

Joseph was a dreamer. He had a dream in which he saw his family bowing down to worship him. That was a very big dream that frightened even his family to the point that they felt they had to do away with him so that those dreams would not come true. You can imagine a poor little boy in the village dreaming of how he became president of the whole country. That is an outrageous dream, but what they didn't understand was that the boy was seeing himself in the future—and eventually that future became a reality. No matter how poor or disadvantaged you may be, if you dream big you will become big one day. In your own private world, see yourself accomplishing big things; imagine yourself a star who is being celebrated, and one day it will come to pass. Dreams are very important because they are the magnet to the future.

Martin Luther King, Jr. had a dream in which he saw the liberty of the black people in a white-dominated nation. That was a big dream at the time considering the circumstances, and today that dream has become the reality that not only are the black people free, one has become the President of the country—something that was thought impossible. Dreams do come true, so go ahead and dream. And make sure it is big enough to make people either laugh at you or think that you are crazy, for it is then that you will know that something great awaits you in the future. If you don't have a dream, find someone who has and help them build their dream; in the process you may be forced to dream your own. There are people walking about today without any money in their pocket but with a great dream, and one day you will be surprised at where they have arrived. Never despise a dreamer, because dreams do come true. If you want to succeed with your gift, dream big, and it will certainly come to pass.

CHAPTER 10

BE OPTIMISTIC

To succeed in life, you must learn to have a positive mindset toward life. You cannot be a pessimist and attract positive things to yourself. If you are positive, you will attract positive energy toward you and things will work for you. No matter how negative things may look, learn to stay positive. Proverbs 23:7 says,

> *For as he thinketh in his heart, so is he....*

As a man thinks so is he. We are all a product of our thoughts. When you think positively, you will succeed; if you think negatively, you will fail. Believe that things will always work out for you no matter how discouraging or negative it may look. Learn to take positive steps. Personally, I have never allowed anything to weigh me down. I always have a positive mindset despite the circumstances of life, and sometimes I feel I was born with a positive mind. I have never thought negatively. I always believe that things will work out for me no matter what; that is why I run away from people who are negative.

I once had an accident, and while my brand new car was somersaulting on the expressway I was not thinking of dying, but was busy thinking of getting the car in for repairs. If the damage were severe, I began to imagine the steps I would take to raise money to buy a new one. Miraculously, I came out of that accident without a scratch, while others sustained injury. When my manager heard and came to the hospital, I asked him to take some pictures of the car and go to the mechanic to get the cost of repairs. It was funny, but that is how I am. When you are optimistic you will become very successful, because positive thoughts and actions attract positive results. Believe that you will become successful no matter how many times you may have failed or been rejected, and soon success will become your friend. To become ten times better than your peers you must be very optimistic, because no one ever accomplishes anything with a negative mindset.

Learn to speak life into your business and career and anything else you do. I knew a girl who did not want to take an exam; when I asked why she said that she felt she would not pass the exam. What a negative mind. She refused to go and take the exam because she saw herself as a failure. You can become a complete failure in life if you have a negative mindset.

That is why God was angry with the spies who were sent to spy out Canaan and returned with negative, discouraging words. They said they would not be able to succeed in their campaign because they saw giants, Numbers 13:31-33.

> *But the men that went up with him said We be not able to go up against the people; for they are stronger than we And they gave the children of Israel a bad report of the land which they had spied out, saying, "The land through which we have gone as spies is a land that devours its inhabitants, and all the people whom we saw in it are men of great stature. There we saw the giants (the descendants of Anak came from the giants); and we were like grasshoppers in our own sight, and so we were in their sight."*

No matter the giants you may see on the way to your Canaan, you must believe that you can overcome them. You must have a positive attitude for success. Many people would have accomplished great things, but they allowed negative thoughts to rule them and so they got stuck in life. To be optimistic is very important if you want to succeed. When you write that proposal, be positive that it will go through. Drop every negative thought; if not, it will draw you back. No matter what you see and no matter how many people may be doing your kind of business, believe that you will be successful, and you will be. Those spies saw giants, and they quickly forgot that God was with them. They gave in to negative thoughts and, because of that, they made others who were looking up to them lose faith and see failure instead of success. To be optimistic means that you believe you will accomplish what you have set yourself to do, and you believe that all things will work for you.

CHAPTER 11

THE POWER OF FOCUS

You must learn to be focused if you plan to succeed. Learn to stay on track and pursue your task. Don't be a jack of all trades and a master of none. When you focus on your business and pursue it with all your energy, you will soon realize how much you have accomplished. Put all your energy into what you are called to do.

> *The light of the body is the eye:*
> *if therefore thine eye be single, thy*
> *whole body shall be full of light.*
> MATTHEW 6:22

Jesus said that if your eye is single, your whole body shall be full of light. To experience the fullness of light, you must keep your eye single. Whatever you have decided to do, stay on course with it so that it can produce the desired result. Don't jump from one thing to another simply because what you started doesn't seem to look promising. Some people are in the habit of jumping into projects in which others are successful, and this always leads to frustration. Focus on your gift. If you are called to be a pastor, don't delve into the shipping business as a part-time job, especially if you are a full-time pastor. This will bring distractions that will harm your success as a pastor. If you discover that your gift is in the music industry, put all your effort in making music, spend time in the studio, write songs or buy some; let all your time and energy be spent on everything that has to do with music, and eventually it will pay off.

I had some friends who loved to play soccer, and they spent their time training and watching football. I used to discourage them from being too involved in football because I thought they would end up without a future. They always came to ask me for money, and I wondered how long that would continue. So I advised them to at least start a business in case soccer didn't work for them, but they refused to listen to me and continued in what they were doing. In fact, their way of dressing changed; every time I saw them they were wearing a jersey. I thought they were insane, but today most of them are playing for international clubs. There is power in focusing on what you are doing without allowing yourself to be distracted, and if you stay focused you will emerge a star.

CHAPTER 12

LOVE WHAT YOU DO

No one will ever appreciate what you do more than yourself. Love what you are cut out to do. Celebrate your business or talent. When you love what you do, people will have to love it, too. You cannot be ashamed of your gift or talent and expect people to appreciate it. No matter what you find yourself doing, love it and enjoy yourself while doing it. I am a born organizer, and I have my own trademark beauty pageant that I organized for seven years. When I started the pageant, people used to laugh at me and call me names. I used to be ashamed to the point that I couldn't even share flyers of the pageant. Then one day a friend noticed and told me if I didn't love what I did and do it with pride, no one else would. Those words got to me, and I had to readjust my thinking and start liking my brand. It then occurred to me that those who laughed at me were doing it out of envy. When I was not with them they asked themselves why they did not come up with such a fine idea as mine. You see, people who may be laughing at you when they see you at your business are doing so out of ignorance or envy, so don't let them make you feel ashamed of what you do. Give all you have to your business or developing your talent, and soon those who laughed will come and celebrate with you.

> *Whatsoever thy hand findeth to do, do it with thy might; for there is no work, nor device, nor knowledge, nor wisdom, in the grave, whither thou goest.*
> ECCLESIASTES 9:10

The scripture says that whatever we find ourselves doing, we should do it with all that is inside of us. When you love what you do, you will do it with all your power and with pride. You will not give room to anyone to ridicule you or look down on you, because it is what you were made to do. When you love what you do, you will do it with joy. There are people who don't love their job, but you find them there every morning. They don't like it, but they can't seem to leave it either. They haven't found themselves yet or they simply don't know what to do with life. Most of the time these people cause the greatest havoc in their working establishment. If you don't love what you do, you will not give it your best. Many times what you love may not be what you were assigned to do in life, and in the long run you will find that you were on the wrong side of life. But when you learn to love what you do—even if you didn't like it at the beginning and it is what you were born to do, you will succeed at it. When you find what you are meant to do, do it with love, protect it, keep and nourish it until it yields fruit.

CHAPTER 13

BELIEVE IN YOURSELF

You can be very positive about life and know that everything will work out well, yet you may not believe in yourself as someone who can accomplish a thing. You may think someone else should do it, and you can only help. To be ten times better than your peers, you need to believe in yourself. Believe that you and only you can do what you are called to do. When you believe in yourself, you will summon enough courage to carry out the task you have at hand. You will have a sense of value and self-worth, and when you have self-worth you will settle for nothing less than the best.

After I finished high school, some friends and I came up with the idea of forming a company in which we would go to local offices in my community and ask for a contract to fumigate their offices against roaches and rats. My friends were excited and everyone was optimistic—that's a great idea and it will work—but when it was time to move, they ran back. None of my friends thought they could do it. They had a positive mindset, but they didn't believe in themselves to do it. You can be positive about life, but you need to believe that you can take the steps to accomplish the job. How many times have you come up with an idea, and your family and friends believed in those ideas but refused to believe in their ability to get those ideas to work? When you believe in yourself courage will come. When you believe in yourself others will believe in you, too. A commander who takes his platoon to the war front must believe in himself or he will lead his troops to death. They may have had great plans and been positive that it would work, but if the commander does not trust in his ability to lead at the front, others will lose faith and the consequences will be disastrous.

CHAPTER 14

THE JOSEPH KIND OF INSIGHT

To be ten times better than your peers, you need the kind of insight that Joseph had. Insight is that certain idea that only you have and others don't. Insight can be defined as the capacity to gain an accurate and deep intuitive understanding, discernment or judgment of something. Those who gained mastery in their business had insight that others did not, and so they became more successful.

Joseph had insight about the state of Egypt and the impending drought, so when he presented it to Pharaoh he was made the Prime Minister. But the interesting thing is that Joseph himself recognized that such insight did not come from him, but from God.

*And Joseph answered Pharaoh, saying,
It is not in me: God shall give Pharaoh
an answer of peace.*
GENESIS 41:16

The Joseph kind of insight, which can set you apart in your field of endeavor, comes only from God. That is why Joseph did not take credit for such discernment, but ascribed praise to God as the source. A brother in my church once gave an outstanding testimony of this Joseph kind of insight. His company had a production machine that stopped working. Expartraits from around the world were called to fix the machine, but they could not. The company became frustrated and did not know what to do. I believe they would have been out of business and possibly laid off their staff if God did not intervene through the brother. While this brother was praying one day God showed him where to press the machine to make it work. When he got to work the following day he told the management that he could fix it; they laughed at him, thinking he was joking. Eventually he was allowed to try; he did what God had showed him and the machine worked. That was insight. The company promoted him to a position he would not have reached on his own in all his years in the company. It is insight that can set you apart and make you very successful.

In 2 Samuel 5:23-24 we see a man of insight who was distinguished in his war career…

And when David enquired of the Lord, he said, Thou shall not go up; but fetch a compass behind them, and come upon them over against the mulberry trees. And let it be, when thou hearest the sound of a going in the tops of the mulberry trees, that then thou shall bestir thyself: for then shall the Lord go out before thee, to smite the host of the Philistines.

David was ten times better than his contemporaries because he had insight that set him apart, and this enabled him to win every war in which he was engaged. God, his source, always showed him what to do, and he can show you, too.

There is a thing some people call a trade secret, but I call it insight. For you to succeed in anything you must have insight about your product that will make people want it. The reason the Coca Cola Company still sells more than any other company in the same business today is because they have a trade secret or insight that they have protected for decades. This has set them apart and made them more successful than the others. Whatever you are called to do, you need insight in order to be distinguished. You need insight to move a struggling business to the next level. The reason some businesses are closed down is because of lack of insight. When you have insight concerning your business, you will be ten times better than those who are doing the same business.

Chapter 15

Mind Your Friends

Those you hang out with in life really matter. There is a saying, "Show me your friends and I will tell you who you are." This is very true, because your friends tell a lot about you. There are two things in life that indicate what you will eventually become—the books you read and the friends you keep. Your friends can either make you or ruin you. The company you keep can make you excel in life or frustrate your future. There are many people who had great destinies who are now in rehabilitation homes, prisons, on the street or in the grave just because of the friends they kept. Despite your great gift or talent, if you keep the wrong friends you will not reach your destination. There are many innocent people in prison who are there because of the friends they kept. They didn't do anything wrong except walk with the wrong company, and most of the time they have no idea what took them to where they find themselves now.

*He that walketh with wise men shall be wise;
but a companion of fools shall be destroyed.*
PROVERBS 13:20

The above passage says that when you walk with wise people you will eventually become wise, but if you keep company with foolish people their foolishness will rub off on you. This suggests that we should be mindful of the kind of friends we keep, because they will have an effect on us. If you associate with successful people, you will learn their ways and soon you will be successful. If you want to get to the height of your career, choose your friends carefully. There are some friends who will not allow you to rise in life. When they see that you are going somewhere great they will talk you down and try to keep you at their level. Some of these friends do it out of envy or fear that you might one day rise above them, and they do not want that to happen.

When you discover your gift and you want to excel in it, keep company with the right people; associate with those who have succeeded in that area or are working to succeed, for with them you will be encouraged to pursue your dream to the end. Remember, your friends are your peers and you want to be ten times better than them, so choose those who will influence you to succeed. If your gift is in track and field and you see yourself becoming the world's fastest man, you should keep friends who are athletes. They will encourage you by waking you up very early in the morning to run miles and do the other training that will make you succeed. But if you keep company with those whose habit it is to spend time in clubs drinking and talking to ladies you are bound to be frustrated, because no drunk ever won an Olympic.

When God wants to bless a man, he always sends a man; therefore be sure the right people are around you, and you will succeed. Not everyone you grew up with has to be around you. Some of your peers are toxic, and if you keep them your future will be spoiled. Many people will come into your life, but you must be wise enough to know who stays and who leaves. You must learn the art of letting some people out of your life. In very rare cases you find two people who were born at the same time in the same neighborhood, attended the same kindergarten and high school, and eventually the same college, who got married, had children, and are still living together in their old age.

At every stage in your life you will meet people; these people have a specific purpose in your life, and when they are done they will leave. You are like a building project—it all starts with the foundation. The first people who come into your life are there to lay the foundation. If you stay with them, your building will never be completed. The second group is the brick layers. This group works very hard in building your life and you may stay long with them, but don't settle with them. The third group is the carpenters who come to install roofing, windows and door panels. At this point in your life if you make the mistake of settling with them, your building will never be completed. These groups of people don't last; they always rush in and rush out.

The fourth group is the electricians. They are the people who come in to install those things that will make your house (life) comfortable. They wire the house so you can have light in the future; they fix the gas pipe and electrical sockets. Never make the mistake of settling with them as some people do, only to regret it later. The fifth group is the painters. Many people make the mistake of settling with this group. The painters are the last group of people in a building project, but they are never the owner of the house. They make your house (life) look beautiful, but it is not for them to live in. Never mistake a painter as the owner of the house.

The true owner of the house may never have contributed to the building of the house; they wait for the house to be finished and walk majestically to take possession of it. If someone leaves you, don't cry; just know the work they came to do is complete and it is time for them to leave so others can begin their own work. You are a building project; don't make the mistake of settling with your workers. Know that when the building is complete, the owner will come irrespective of how long it took to build the house. I heard someone once say, "I labored for him, and when it was time he didn't want me anymore." You don't have to cry a river; you were there to help build that life. Sometimes, and on many occasions, a smart worker can take possession of the house, depending on his capabilities.

Be mindful of your friends, for they are the very measurement of your success in life. Don't mistake proximity with love and affection. The people you grew up with in your neighborhood may not necessarily be the ones you should be close to. Your true companion may be somewhere far away, but you only have to behave like Peter, who acted on the instructions of Jesus to launch out into the deep. Cast your net right into the deep far away from your peers, and you will have a net-breaking catch of quality people who will help decorate your life. According to Luke 5:4,

> *Now when he had left speaking, he said*
> *unto Simon, Launch out into the deep,*
> *and let down your nets for a draught.*

You must learn to leave your comfort zone and go where your peers are not. The reason some people cannot succeed is because they are too tied to where they were born or brought up. The people they call family, friends and neighbors are the reason for their stagnation. You have to break free in order to succeed. Many people are like Abraham in the Bible, who was so attached to his parents and relatives that he couldn't succeed in life—until God intervened by asking him to leave his father's house and go out to find a life. Abraham had a great destiny, but being too attached to the people he grew up with almost destroyed that destiny. He couldn't do without his family; even when he left, he still carried one relative along with him in the person of Lot (Genesis 12). How can you be 30 years of age and still living with your parents; until you leave you will not succeed.

There are some people you meet who, if you keep them as friends, will make your life miserable. In Psalm 1:1-3,

> *Blessed is the man that walketh not in the counsel of the ungodly, nor standeth in the way of sinners, nor sitteth in the seat of the scornful. But his delight is in the law of the Lord; and in his law doth he meditate day and night. And he shall be like a tree planted by the rivers of water, that bringeth forth his fruit in his season; his leaf also shall not wither; and whatever he doeth shall prosper.*

The above scripture shows us what bad friends can to our destiny. If you want to be a blessed and successful individual, do not walk in the counsel of ungodly people. This means that you should not fashion your life according to the advice of the wrong friends. Do not keep company with those who do wrong things, and run away from people whose business is to laugh at others who are trying to fulfill their destiny. Make friends with God's word, and keep company with people who will encourage you to go to church and also help you to fulfill your destiny. Then you shall be like a tree planted by the rivers of water, and you will make progress and produce tangible results every season.

The friends we keep are really important, because some people can bring destruction into your life. With some people you meet you can lose everything you ever worked for and perhaps even lose your life if care is not taken. As in the case of Jonah in Jonah 1:1-17, because of his actions those who were around him lost all their property and almost lost their lives. There are some friends who are like Achan in the Bible (Joshua 7). When you meet them your life will become a mess; they will pull you back and eventually make you lose your life. There are also people who will bring sunshine and blessings into your life, much like Joseph and Potiphar in Genesis 39:3 and Jacob and Laban in Genesis 30:27-30.

Avoid toxic friends; choose carefully whom you want to be friends with, and let it be predicated upon their ability to help you succeed in life. Learn to sit down and ask yourself "what has this friendship added to my life?" If a friend or relationship does not add any value to your life, then end it. You should not attend some churches, because they will ruin your destiny through their wrong prophecies and ill advice. Some will tell you that God wants you to marry a certain person only for you to regret later. If God wants to reveal whom you should marry, he will not show it to your pastor or church member, but you. Ask God to direct you; he says in Jeremiah 3:15,

And I will give you pastors according to mine heart, which shall feed you with knowledge and understanding.

Every man has a pastor assigned to him; until you meet that pastor you may be struggling with fulfilling your purpose. That is why you hear some people say that as soon as they went to a particular church their life changed, while others feel the urge to leave where they are worshiping. The wrong church is like toxic friends, and you should be as mindful of this as you are mindful of your friends.

CHAPTER 16

AVOID TIME WASTERS

To succeed in life and be ten times better than your peers, you must avoid time wasters. This is one area in which people struggle despite their big dreams and talents. There are many things that can make you lose valuable time that should have been invested in your future. Most of the time this happens without our being aware that it is destructive. These things can ruin your future and eventually your greatness if you are not careful. They range from unnecessary phone calls to spending time on social media and television to unproductive visits with friends and relatives. Time wasters hinder productivity, and you must close your door any time you see them. Most of us spend too much time on the phone talking trash when we should be using that time in doing things that will benefit our life. We spend a great amount of time on the phone telling stories, and sometimes if we don't have anything to say we switch to songs and sometimes keep quiet, but we're still on the phone without saying anything. Try using that time in productive thinking if you have nothing to do; you will be surprised what you may come up with.

In this age of Facebook, Instagram, Twitter and Whats Up, we are faced with numerous distractions that have ruined many destinies. People spend countless valuable hours through these media, and they make life very unproductive. Unless you have a business that requires you to be on social media, you should not waste your time going through them. You can't be going for a morning workout as an athlete or boxer, and the greater part of the hour you are tweeting on Twitter. Instead of checking the menu to see what creative meal you may have to cook as a chef, you spend your morning hours taking selfies that will add nothing valuable or cause a television station to call you to cook on their show. Other time wasters are unnecessary visits with friends and relations, especially in your workplace and home. They come in with no genuine reason but to distract you from doing what you are supposed to be doing. Some come in with useless talk, and before you know it the day has ended and you have nothing to show that you achieved that day.

Every day of your life should be productive; you should do something that will add to your future. That time you wasted with friends and relatives in useless talk or on social media could have been channeled into writing that book, enrolling in that class or planning that big event that will showcase your abilities.

Television may be the best way to reach out to people in advertising products and services, but it is the number one enemy of man's productivity. Some people are so addicted to television that their career, business and family suffer for this addiction. Spending too much time on television at home or at work can ruin your entire life and is the number one time waster. Television is good, but when it takes your time away from doing your assignment it becomes evil. You must learn to cut down on some of your television shows and invest that time in your future. Sometimes when I spend too much time watching television I realize that those people on the show have been paid and the producers have made their money already, and maybe even as I am watching they are on location filming another one. This makes me jump up and go do my own thing so that others can see my work tomorrow. One of the things I choose to do instead of wasting time on TV is working on this book you are reading now.

Sleep is a serious time waster and it has made a lot of people poor. The Bible warns about it in Proverbs 24:33-34…

Yet a little sleep, a little slumber,
a little folding of the hands to sleep:
So shall thy poverty come as one that
travelleth; and thy want as an armed man.

Sleep can ruin your career and business; it is the best friend of the poor. Sleep is a serious time waster. When you should be up and doing you will just submit to the urge to sleep, and before you know it time has gone and you accomplished nothing. If you want to succeed, you must avoid unnecessary sleep.

Avoid time wasters; run from them. Anything that you know will take your time away from doing what you should be doing or pursuing your purpose should be avoided. Don't let anyone or anything distract you from fulfilling your dream.

CHAPTER 17

OVERCOME PEER PRESSURE

Peer pressure is one of the things we must overcome if we want to succeed in life. You cannot be ten times better than your peers if you are still influenced by your peers. Your peers constitute one of the greatest influences in your life, and you must learn to overcome them in order to rise above them. Your peers are the people you grew up with, your classmates or your friends you spend a great deal of time with. Many great destinies have been destroyed because of pressures put on them by their peers. If you are not careful your peers will pressure you into drugs, prostitution, gangs and even robbery. If you give in to them, you might end up with incurable diseases, become a junkie or even die, and I don't think anyone in these categories can become ten times better than their peers except by the mercy of God. The Bible in the book of Proverbs 1:10 warns,

My son, if sinners entice thee,
consent thou not.

When your peers mount pressure on you to do something that is contrary to the will of God for your life, do not consent to them. Be aware that most times your peers act out of envy. They can pressure you to wear certain designer clothes that you may not have the money for at the time, and to please them you begin to involve yourself in something destructive. In Romans 12:2 the scripture says,

And be not conformed to this world:
but be ye transformed by the renewing of your
mind, that ye may prove what is that good,
and acceptable, and perfect, will of God.

You don't have to conform to your peers' way of doing things, but you must transform your mind and pay no attention to them. Spend time with your work; give it everything you've got and pay no mind to what anyone may say to the contrary. Your peers may taunt you because you always go to church, dress decently or read the Bible whenever you are less busy. Don't mind them; instead, mind your future. When you overcome peer pressure you will develop a sense of confidence, and this will help you in achieving your purpose.

Chapter 18

Stand Out

On your way to success, you must stand out from the crowd. Be yourself; everyone else is taken. Cut out a niche for yourself. You are an original copy, so stop forcing yourself to become a photocopy.

> *Wherefore come out from among them, and be ye separate, saith the Lord, and touch not the unclean thing; and I will receive you.*
> 2 Corinthians 6:17

The Bible says that you should come out from among them. You don't need to be like everyone else; you must strive to be different. Do your things differently, and set your own path for others to follow. Be unique in your own way and learn to be comfortable with who you are. Let it be that people will notice when you are not there, because there is something distinct about you. Come out of the norm and do things the way you believe they should be done. Sometimes it is not easy to stand out, because some people will hate you just because you are different. When Jesus came to this earth, the people who were supposed to work with him were the ones who hated him and eventually killed him, because he was different. If you cut out a niche for yourself and decide to be different you will face lots of persecution, but this should not deter you. It should only make you understand that you are different, and people are not comfortable with it. Apostle Paul was a killer; he got the license to kill Christians. But when Jesus appeared to him in Acts 9, he stood up and became the greatest of the apostles; he was hated and almost stoned to death. As you discover your gift and begin to work in actualizing it, do your things differently and avoid being a copycat. Let people know you for who you are. There is a great distinction between McDonalds and KFC. Even when they are on the same corner of the street they make sales because each of them is distinct. Let your businesses stand out; be creatively different from others so that even when you are with others who have the same business or talent, you can easily stand out.

CHAPTER 19

REFUSE TO COMPROMISE

On your way to success, set a high standard for yourself and refuse to compromise no matter what. The moment you decide to compromise means you have decided to fail, because compromise is like a virus that eats deep—and when you least expect it everything comes crumbling down. Don't strike a balance or give and take just to succeed. You don't have to sleep with anyone in order to make it in life or give bribe. There is no shortcut or middle ground for success. Every corporation or business that succeeds most oftentimes has set a high standard for the business, and anyone who tries to compromise the standard pays the price of expulsion.

When you discover your gift and begin to work on becoming successful in it, set a high standard and refuse to compromise. Have a personal code or principles that no one can talk you out of. If you are a soccer player, your personal time of training should not be compromised with anything, because it is your connection to the success of your career in soccer. If you compromise your personal training time with some other things that don't really matter to your calling, when the time comes for selection to a national team or foreign base clubs, you may be found wanting and your future in soccer will be bleak. The same is applicable to all areas of life. If you are going to succeed, don't compromise your principles of success that you set for yourself, but follow them to a logical conclusion no matter how stupid it may look or sound to people around you.

Sometimes the things you do to succeed may not sound right to people, but it doesn't matter. What matters is the results you will get. I used to wake up at twelve midnight to pray until 1:00 am and, whenever I woke up to pray, two people who were with me in the house always looked at me like I was crazy or just wasting my time, but that is my principle. That hour of the night is too critical for me to talk to any human; instead let me use it to talk to God. Eventually it paid off; I am ten times better than those who were with me then. Refuse to compromise your principles of success and you will be more successful than your peers.

CHAPTER 20

GET A MENTOR

There is no self-made man. There is no star who made it on their own; every great and winning team has a great coach. You cannot take the journey of life alone and expect to be successful. God made this clear in Genesis 2:18...

> *And the Lord God said, It is not good that the man should be alone; I will make him an help meet for him.*
> AND IN ECCLESIASTES 4:9-10
>
> *Two are better than one; because they have a great reward for their labour. For if they fall, the one will lift up his fellow: but woe to him that is alone when he falleth; for he hath not another to help him up.*

There is no one who can succeed on their own; everyone needs help, and God said he will provide a help suitable for your destiny. There is someone out there who can help you become all that you were created to be. I have read through the Bible and have not seen anyone who made it on their own. If you truly want to be ten times better than your peers, you must look for those who will stretch you and not those who will limit you. There is a saying that "if you want to go fast go alone, but if you want to go far go with someone." Going fast doesn't mean you have gone far; you need someone who will help you to go far in life.

A mentor is someone who guides a less experienced person. A mentor is a helper who provides constructive and positive information and ideas based on their experiences to encourage another. A mentor helps you to see possibilities.

> *Thus saith the Lord, Stand ye in the ways, and see, and ask for the old paths, where is the good way, and walk therein, and ye shall find rest for your souls. But they said, We will not walk therein.*
> JEREMIAH 6:16

God says you should ask for the old path. Find out how to make it from those who have made it. There is an old path which, when you take it, can lead to success. When I hear some people say they are a self-made man, I take it to be foolish, because whatever they did to succeed they learned from someone else.

There is an old path that you can follow if you want to be like those who were before you. There is nothing new under the sun; there are just different ways of approach that bring different results. No matter your dreams or ideas, someone else has had them, and you can tap into their resources to become great. If you follow someone great, you can always be greater than them. Jesus said you should follow him and greater works than these shall you do. So if you follow Jesus you have made him your mentor, and you can do greater things than he did when he was on the earth.

> *And he saith unto them, Follow me,*
> *and I will make you fishers of men.*
> MATTHEW 4:19

> *Verily, verily, I say unto you, He that*
> *believeth on me, the works that I do shall*
> *he do also; and greater works than these*
> *shall he do; because I go unto my Father.*
> JOHN 14:12

You can be ten times better than your peers in your business, career, marriage and academics if you follow those who made it in that area.

> *That ye be not slothful, but followers*
> *of them who through faith and patience*
> *inherit the promises.*
> HEBREWS 6:12

Mind you, it is not everyone whom you must follow. Getting a mentor does not mean that you follow in the footsteps of just any kind of person whom you think is successful. The scripture says you should follow after those with traceable success and proven integrity, those who made it genuinely. In Matthew 11:29, Jesus our mentor said, "Take my yoke upon you, and learn of me; for I am meek and lowly in heart: and ye shall find rest unto your souls." A mentor will show you where to put your legs and how to go about what you intend to do; he will let you know the secret to the success of your given task. Without a mentor, you may be like a sheep without a shepherd, going through life without a proper guide. Apostle Paul was a mentor to Timothy and Timothy succeeded; if you want to succeed, get a mentor.

CHAPTER 21

THE POWER OF MEDITATION

Meditation is the life wire to success. There is absolute power in meditation. If you want to climb to the highest height in your business and career, you must learn the art of meditation. Meditation is the art of chewing on the word of God to get the juice out of it and the juice is what we eventually call revelation. When you catch a revelation on the word, it means you have been adequately lighted in that area and when you are lighted, you begin to dominate that particular area of life. God advises us to meditate if we want to succeed in life; see Joshua 1:8...

> *This book of the law shall not depart out of thy mouth; but thou shalt **meditate** therein day and night, that thou mayest observe to do according to all that is written therein: for then thou shalt make thy way prosperous, and then thou shalt have **good success**.*

Good success comes from meditating on the word of God. To meditate, you center your mind and thoughts on a particular word of God concerning a particular area of your life. You keep contemplating, brooding and reflecting on the word until something is revealed to you from that word. Many of us read the Bible on the surface, and oftentimes the little results we get from such reading are like picking nuggets from the shore. But genuine treasures come from deep meditation, which we have to do day and night. If, for example, you want to pass at the top of your class, there is a word in the Bible concerning that in Psalm 119:99:

> *I have more understanding than all my teachers:*
> *for thy testimonies are my meditation.*

And another scripture in Deuteronomy 28:13 says…

> *And the Lord shall make thee the head,*
> *and not the tail; and thou shalt be above*
> *only, and thou shalt not be beneath; if that*
> *thou hearken unto the commandments of*
> *the Lord thy God, which I command thee*
> *this day, to observe and to do them.*

You can meditate on these scriptures that talk about success, and suddenly you catch a revelation that will put you at the top of your class. If you invest the time in meditation that you use in thinking about money or your friends, you will rise above the circumstance that is trying to weigh you down. We see a man in the Bible who became ten times better than his contemporaries because of meditation. This man was Isaac.

> *Then Isaac sowed in that land, and received in the same year an hundredfold: and the Lord blessed him. And the man waxed great, and went forward, and grew until he became very great.*
> GENESIS 26:12-13

Isaac became very great even in the time of famine. While people were running to Egypt for greener pastures, God told Isaac to stay where he was and sow, and the result was amazing. But this blessing did not come casually, because it is recorded in Genesis 24:63 that Isaac always went to meditate.

> *And Isaac went out to meditate in the field at the eventide: and he lifted up his eyes, and saw, and, behold, the camels were coming.*

I believe it was in the place of meditation that God revealed to him the secret of success. The scripture also says in Psalm 1:2,

But his delight is in the law of the Lord; and in his law doth he meditate day and night.

While you are meditating, God can reveal secrets to your success that will set you apart and make you ten times better than your peers.

Chapter 22

Dress to Be Addressed

The way you dress matters even more than the dream you have. There is a story of a young man who graduated from high school but did not have a job, so he decided to become a con man. He bought very good clothes and dressed properly as though his father were a billionaire. This young man lied his way to the White House, and the President of the United State welcomed him with a Presidential handshake and photo ops. By this time everyone knew who he was; he was already at the top, recognized even by the President and had gained access to most of the celebrities in the country. You don't have to inquire about the authenticity of the story, but try to get the benefit of it. What got the young man to the top was the way he dressed; wherever he went, doors were opened to him because of his appearance.

If you want doors to open to you, too, you must learn to dress well. People will always address you depending on the way you are dressed. You cannot be ten times better than your peers dressing like a thug. I have never seen a President giving audience to some guy with sagging pants and piercings everywhere. You must look responsible in order to attract responsible people your way. If you have a big dream but your appearance does not match your dream, you are in for a long delay in life. Earlier in my life I organized a beauty pageant, and I wore a dreadlock. I thought I looked cool with it until I went to the bank to ask for a partnership for the next edition of the beauty pageant. The proposal was good and inviting, and the bank was interested, but my appearance was not welcome. Finally, the bank manager told this to my friend, who told me that I couldn't come to the bank requesting hundreds of thousands of dollars looking like a thug. They said they liked the pageant and the proposal, but they were not comfortable with my appearance. I lost a big partnership that year, but I learned a lesson.

You see, you may think that your project is wonderful and that no one will ever reject it, but I want to tell you that you matter more than the project. People will always buy the seller of the product before they buy the product. You must invest in making yourself saleable before you launch your product. We all hear of Oprah, but most people don't know what Oprah does to make money or how she became a household name. She did a good job of selling herself until she became an institution. If people don't like you they will not buy your product, so market yourself by the way you appear. The story of Joseph in the Bible, who goes from prison to a palace, shows that the way you dress matters. In Genesis 41:14 it is recorded that Joseph shaved himself and changed his clothes; if not, he would not have been accepted into the palace. And even if he were accepted, the king would never have given him any post because he didn't look good before him.

Dress properly every time you leave your house. Ask yourself if you can travel the way you are dressed to another country or if you could attend a function like that without having to rush home and change. As a lady, always ask yourself if you were the wife of a President, would you dress like that. If you have never attracted responsible men, you may not look responsible enough. Like attracts like. Your kind will always locate you. Your dream of becoming a president or congressman may not come true if you continue to wear saggy pants. You must learn to appear as a gentleman, and gentlemen will locate you. Have you not noticed that anytime you dress nicely people compliment you, and behind you they may be asking someone, "Who is that gentleman?" Every time you dress properly you are giving yourself the opportunity to succeed, because you never know whom you will meet.

> *But put ye on the Lord Jesus Christ,*
> *and make not provision for the flesh,*
> *to fulfil the lusts thereof.*
> ROMANS 13:14

Let your dressing reflect the nature of Jesus. Your body may want to dress like the people you see in the world, but the Bible advises you not to give in to it. Let it be that anytime people see you, they see the glory of God in you through your dressing. Remember, you are always addressed according to the way you dress.

CHAPTER 23

RELEASE YOUR ANGELS

If you want to be ten times better than your peers, you must learn to make use of your angels. There are paths you may never cross in life, and there are heights you may never reach, without angelic intervention. God has a plan to take you to the highest of high in life, but this can only be fulfilled through the help of your angels. Before Jesus could succeed in his ministry and finally sit at the right hand of majesty on high—with a name that is above every other name on the earth, showing that he is ten times better than his peers—he was marvelously helped by his angels.

Then the devil leaveth him, and, behold, angels came and ministered unto him.
MATTHEW 4:11

And there appeared an angel unto him from heaven, strengthening him.
LUKE 22:43

You must understand that everyone who is born into this world has an angel attached to them until a certain age, according to Matthew 18:10:

> *Take heed that ye despise not one of*
> *these little ones; for I say unto you,*
> *That in heaven their angels do always behold*
> *the face of my Father which is in heaven.*

And when that person comes to full realization of self and has to choose between good and evil, if he makes a choice to serve God, angels will be released to attend to him according to his purpose. The job of the angels is to bring the word of God to work in the life of that individual. But if you reject Jesus and serve the devil, your angels are withdrawn. God doesn't waste his resources.

Now, many believers don't know that there is an invisible companion who goes with them everywhere. They see what you do and take account of everything concerning you. But many people don't use them. You have to learn to release your angels. You can send your angels to work for you. You can ask them to fight your battles and also open doors that have been shut against you. This is their ministry. Many believers are suffering unnecessarily without knowing that there is a company of angels that goes everywhere with them if only they knew how to send them.

> *And he answered, Fear not: for they that be
> with us are more than they that be with them.*
> 2 Kings 6:16

Every child of God has a guardian angel who has been with them right from birth. That guardian angel was there right from the moment you were conceived; he made sure you were kept well in the womb, and when you were born he protected you until you were fully grown and made sure no evil came upon you. You can never outgrow your angel. And apart from your personal guardian angel, you have a company of angels assigned to you to help you succeed, but you have a duty to command them in line with the word of God to work for you. Where you are met with a roadblock on your way to success, you have to release the angels to clear the road for you. They are always waiting for your command; if you don't command them they will just be staring at you. Many of us carry too many loads that tend to weigh us down in our journey of life, when we have angels who are always on standby to help us.

Like many of us in life who are faced with obstacles on our way to success, there was a man in the Bible who was faced with a great obstacle on the way to taking his people to their Canaan. This obstacle was the Wall of Jericho, which was the strongest and most impregnable fortress on the earth at the time, but help came through angels who came to their aid.

> *And it came to pass, when Joshua was by Jericho, that he lifted up his eyes and looked, And, behold, there stood a man over against him with his sword drawn in his hand: and Joshua went unto him, and said unto him, Art thou for us, or for our adversaries? And he said, Nay; but as captain of the host of the Lord am I now come. And Joshua fell on his face to the earth, and did worship, and said unto him, What saith my Lord unto his servant?*
>
> JOSHUA 5:13-14

Thank God that Joshua was able to see the help that was made available to him, and with that help Jericho was leveled and their breakthrough secured. You must understand that no matter how spiritual or anointed you are, you need the ministry of angels in order to succeed in your assignment. Anointing, no matter how great, cannot replace the ministry of angels, else Jesus would not have needed any. Whatever you are called to do in life, you must engage your angels in order to succeed. As a believer, you are more advantaged than your peers because of the angels at your disposal.

I was owed money in my business, and when I approached my debtors they refused to pay. One day God opened my eyes to the ministry of angels, and so with the knowledge I acquired about their operation, I began to release them to go and collect my debts. Surprisingly, the very next day all of them called me and with apology paid me to the very last dollar that I was owed.

Angels work. They can carry your file and make whomever is responsible see it and give you that promotion you have been expecting for years. They can help you in your talent and gift and make you succeed. They can guide you through that proposal and make you get that desired contract. They can help you in sports and music and make you a star. Surely they can help you succeed.

CHAPTER 24

INTEGRITY

Honesty is the best policy. In all your dealings maintain your integrity; do not cut corners just to make it in life. Avoid the urge to get rich and famous quickly or die trying. Don't dupe people or exercise fraud to get rich, because it won't last. And even when it seems like it is going to last, you will not live in peace; if you want to know the truth ask those engaging in it. If you are dubious, sooner or later the strong arm of the law of both God and man will catch up with you, and you will pay the price to the full extent of the law both in life and the afterlife.

Integrity is the quality of being honest, having strong moral principles and moral uprightness. It is a state of being whole and undivided. The scripture says in Proverbs 22:1:

> *A good name is rather to be chosen*
> *than great riches, and loving favour*
> *rather than silver and gold.*

To have a good name, the Bible says, is better than great riches. If you acquire riches by fraud, you have spoiled your name; that will rub off on your family because people will not want to be associated with you. Having a bad name is like having bad credit; you can't get anything with it. There have been many rich men who left a bad name for their family, and because of that the family cannot get any good things because nobody wants to deal with them. Remember that anything you have in life will soon fade away, including you, but your name will remain.

The prophet Samuel was a man of integrity, and one day he did a remarkable thing to prove his integrity. We see in 1 Samuel 12:3-5:

> *Behold, here I am: witness against me before the Lord, and before his anointed: whose ox have I taken? or whose ass have I taken? or whom have I defrauded? whom have I oppressed? or of whose hand have I received any bribe to blind mine eyes therewith? And I will restore it you. And they said, thou hast not defrauded us, nor oppressed us, neither hast thou taken ought of any man's hand. And he said unto them, the Lord is witness against you, and his anointed is witness this day, that ye have not found ought in my hand. And they answered, He is witness.*

That was a man of integrity. Despite the important position he held, he did not soil his hand; that is why we still talk about him today. Unfortunately, it is difficult to find men of integrity today. People do all kinds of dubious things just to make it in life, even in the body of Christ. You cannot do business with some fellow Christians without their trying to cheat you; some even go to the extent of trying to kill just to possess everything. If you lend a fellow Christian money, they find it very difficult to pay it back. People who hold titles in church and are entrusted with counting church money every Sunday are in the habit of stealing church money to enrich themselves, and yet they want to be successful in life. We see pastors sleeping with female members of the church, and some do it with impunity, not minding who is noticing them, as if that were part of their ministry. Men of God whom God sent to go and rescue souls are now making themselves rich with church money that they took by force and not by right. The Bible says in Proverbs 13:11,

> *Wealth gotten by vanity shall be diminished:*
> *but he that gathereth by labour shall increase.*
> AND IN JEREMIAH 17:11:

> *As the partridge sitteth on eggs, and hatcheth them not; so he that getteth riches, and not by right, shall leave them in the midst of his days, and at his end shall be a fool.*

If you dupe people or steal church money, that money will diminish or you will die and leave them. You don't have to play pranks to get rich. You can become wealthy if you follow God's principles, and little by little you will become rich.

The fastest and most secure way to becoming successful and ten times better than your peers is to maintain your integrity. Avoid anything that will dent your name. Never take what does not belong to you. Don't take enhancement drugs to participate in sports. Don't lie about your age in order to be accepted. Be clean inside out, and your star will shine. Whatever name you build for yourself will have a reverberating effect on your generation. So if you steal to make it, or kill to make it, your children will suffer for it.

> *The just man walketh in his integrity: his children are blessed after him.*
> PROVERBS 20:7

What we do in life echoes in eternity. If you are a person of integrity, it will reflect on your children and your next generations. Your actions now either rewrite what is in your lineage or ruin it. In whatever things you are entrusted, maintain your integrity so that it can be well with you and the generations after you. Let your yes be yes, and your no, no. Don't say one thing and do another. Let your words and your deeds be the same. Know that your future depends largely on your integrity and not your gift. The foundation of people trusting you is your integrity. Do not receive or give bribes. Don't steal from your job; don't lie to get days off work. Be honest and discipline yourself. You don't need anyone to monitor you if you are a person of integrity. Many times we lose good relationships that would have helped our destiny because of lack of integrity.

Integrity and holiness are one and the same thing. If you are a man of integrity it means you are holy, and being holy means you are one with yourself, that you don't live a double life. You don't say one thing and do another even in secret. God is a God of integrity, and the scripture says he is Holy and never changes.

> *For I am the Lord, I change not;*
> *therefore ye sons of Jacob are not consumed.*
> MALACHI 3:6

Another scripture says in Psalm 89:35:

> *Once have I sworn by my holiness*
> *that I will not lie unto David.*

And another one says in James 1:17:

Every good gift and every perfect gift is from above, and cometh down from the Father of lights, with whom is no variableness, neither shadow of turning.

The above scriptures clearly tell the true character of God, that he is a man of integrity. God doesn't say one thing and do another; that is why everyone calls upon him and believes in his word. Even those who don't believe in his existence unconsciously call upon him for help because he is true to himself. There are many people who profess one thing and do another. They preach about sanctity, but in their secret lives they violate the very principles they set before others. There are people who are supposedly men of integrity, but if you entrust them with power or money they turn into something else. There is a saying that if you want to know the true nature of a man, give him power. This is very true, because the true character of a man will come out if you give him more money than he ever imagined or you put him in a position of authority. Integrity is a must if you want to succeed in life and be ten times better than your peers.

CHAPTER 25

An Attitude of Thanksgiving

Thanksgiving is a spiritual dynamics for increase. The reason many people experience stagnation or stunted growth in their endeavors is because they have refused to give thanks to God for his blessings upon their life. Many people are very ungrateful even for the little that God has blessed them with, and because of that they cannot rise above their present level. When you thank God for the little, he will multiply it. If you are not a thanks giver, you will certainly be a murmurer. Thanksgiving helps us to overcome murmuring and complaining.

When you give a gift to someone and they look at you with eyes of ingratitude you feel very bad, but if they show appreciation you will be moved to give more. The same goes with God; if you don't appreciate him for the little he will not respond with an increase.

Jesus our savior had a situation when there was a need to feed 5,000 hungry people. The disciples brought five loaves and two fishes with complaint, saying, "What are these among so many?" Jesus, knowing the implication of such an attitude, quickly took that seemingly small provision, lifted it up to heaven and gave thanks to God. The result of that was the feeding of 5,000, which we learn in John 6:5-12.

As you start out on the journey of developing your gifts or managing that small business, you must learn to give thanks to God all along the way. Do not compare yourself with your friends who have gone ahead of you, and begin to complain. If you acknowledge God at every step you take he can help you to overtake those who were ahead of you. When you make thanksgiving a lifestyle, you have opened the door of increase in your life. Many people are looking for an explosive breakthrough in their life before they thank God, but they forget the little things that God is doing in their life every day. You may be looking for a breakthrough, but God sees that if that breakthrough comes it will destroy you because certain things were not cleared out first. So he works to clear those things which you cannot see, but you are there complaining. If God were to open your eyes to see the battle against your life and how he has been fighting on your behalf, you would thank him every minute of your existence. When you have a great destiny, your battles in life will be very great. The reason why you are alive today and still breathing is a clear fact that God is fighting for you. There are many of your peers in the grave, a mortuary, a hospital bed with terminal diseases, prison houses and rehabilitation homes. Some are kidnapped and cannot be found, but you are alive. You must show some appreciation by giving God thanks for his mercies. No matter how things may not be working at the pace you desire, no matter how many times you have been disappointed and your dreams seems farfetched, you must give thanks to God. When you do this in any situation, God will turn everything around for good for you.

> *In every thing give thanks: for this is the will of God in Christ Jesus concerning you.*
> 1 Thessalonian 5:18

Many people have misinterpreted this passage to mean that any circumstance in your life is the will of God, so you should give thanks. That is why in every instance of an evil happening they say it is God's will. No, this passage means that it is God's will for you to give thanks. Thanksgiving is God's will; even when you have not arrived at your destination yet, give thanks. That situation may not be the will of God for you, but do his will by giving thanks. We have all made many mistakes in life. We may be paying the price for choices we have made that were not God's will for our life. But when we give thanks, which is doing his will, God can step in and turn that situation to work for our good.

The fastest way to make it in life is by living a thanksgiving lifestyle. When you thank God for the good things in your life you are invariably ascribing glory to him, which indicates you have seen that you could not have achieved that without God's help. God hates murmurers and complainers. If you are not a thanks giver you will be a murmurer, and if you are a murmurer you attract God's wrath.

Neither murmur ye, as some of them also murmured, and were destroyed of the destroyer.
1 CORINTHIANS 10:10

When you are not grateful to God for the things he has done for you, you displease him and then attract the destroyer to your life. In Numbers 11:1:

And when the people complained, ***it displeased*** *the Lord: and the Lord heard it; and his anger was kindled; and the fire of the Lord burnt among them, and consumed them that were in the uttermost parts of the camp.*

Thanksgiving can save us a lot of trouble. To me, it is more cost effective to be thankful. God loves those who are grateful, and he always multiplies their blessings beyond doubt. Therefore, learn to appreciate what God has done and what he is doing for you—and you will see him take you to your high place in life and make you ten times better than your peers.

CHAPTER 26

COVENANT PRACTICE

Covenant practice is the highway to greatness. You cannot reap if you don't sow. No matter how great your gift, if you are not a giver you will not get anywhere great in life. You may do anything else in the world to make it in life and pay the price when the law catches up with you, but if you want to be successful according to the principles of the kingdom you must be a seed sower.

Covenant practice in this context connotes paying of tithes, offerings and other investments to promote the course of the kingdom. To begin with, we will look at tithing. Tithing is the most important aspect of kingdom investment, because it is the only one that comes with a promise and security. God promised to rebuke the devourer for our sake if we pay our tithe.

> *Bring ye all the tithes into the storehouse, that there may be meat in mine house, and prove me now herewith, saith the Lord of hosts, if I will not open you the windows of heaven, and pour you out a blessing, that there shall not be room enough to receive it. And I will rebuke the devourer for your sakes, and he shall not destroy the fruits of your ground; neither shall your vine cast her fruit before the time in the field, saith the Lord of hosts.*
> MALACHI 3:10-11

We should understand that every other giving may bring returns, but it is only the tithe that promises security for our returns. Tithing is ten percent of our total income. It is the gross and not the net. Your tithe is paid from the total amount of your income before any deduction is made. If you pay your tithe after deductions are made, you are only deceiving yourself, because it is not recorded in heaven and that money is lost. In paying your tithe, you must do it faithfully before you can experience the blessing that comes with it. If you pay your tithes intermittently, that is, whenever you like or whenever you can, you will not experience any blessing. The scripture says bring all the tithe, and this means that it must be done all the time. Your entire income in a year must be tithed. Since you are not paid yearly, but weekly or monthly, you must consistently bring your tithe to the storehouse year in and year out.

God's prosperity plan is not a promise, so it does not answer to prayer; it is not a promise, so it has no respect for fasting. God's prosperity plan is a covenant; if your part is not played, God is not committed, according to Bishop David Oyedepo. If you want to prosper and be ten times better than your peers, you must be an addicted tither. Your tithe is for your local assembly where you are fed spiritually; therefore to do it correctly you must locate a place of worship. There you can sow your seed of tithing, and your increase will meet you right there.

> *Take heed to thyself that thou offer not thy burnt offerings in every place that thou seest: But in the place which the Lord shall choose in one of thy tribes, there thou shalt offer thy burnt offerings, and there thou shalt do all that I command thee.*
> DEUTERONOMY 12:13-14

There is a place to sow and there is a method on how to do it; when you tithe correctly the windows of heaven are open to you and devourers are rebuked on your behalf. The windows of heaven spoken of in the above scripture mean divine ideas. You see, in every endeavor you need ideas to excel. In your gifting, you need ideas to excel more than others who are in that field. By reason of tithing, God can give you an idea that will cause you to become a celebrity in that area. The rain of ideas can only come through tithing. If you pray until you become red in the face and fast until you die, if you are not a tither you will never experience the windows of heaven or see the devourer rebuked on your behalf.

There are many people who we think are very successful, but if they were to open up to us about their predicament we would never seek to measure up with people, but do only the word of God. The next aspect of covenant practice is offerings and other giving. The Bible says we should not appear before God empty handed, Exodus 34:20 and Deuteronomy 16:16. In every worship service, you must carry something in your hand to present to God, and when you give it shall be given back to you in full measure.

> *Give, and it shall be given unto you; good measure, pressed down, and shaken together, and running over, shall men give into your bosom. For with the same measure that ye mete withal it shall be measured to you again.*
> LUKE 6:38

We can also give for church projects either announced in church or as led by God. We can give to our pastors; this is called prophet's offering, and the Bible says when we give to a prophet we will receive a prophet's reward (Matthew 10:41).

Engagement in covenant practice is the most secure path to our fulfilling of glorious destiny. Giving is sowing, and when we sow we will certainly reap. Without covenant practice, there will be no platform for God to reach out to us in blessing the works of our hands. If we engage in these principles, we will rise above every circumstance, succeed in our entire life endeavor and become ten times better than our peers, for this is the secret to greatness.

CHAPTER 27

KINGDOM SERVICE

Kingdom service means to work for God, and working for God means that you are working for the most generous employer on the earth. God is not a task master. God pays more than any establishment on the earth. When you engage in kingdom service you have made God your employer, and your pay is always guaranteed. In Exodus 23:25-26, the packages for kingdom service are enumerated:

> *And ye shall serve the Lord your God, and he shall **bless thy bread, and thy water**; and I will **take sickness away** from the midst of thee. There shall **nothing cast their young, nor be barren**, in thy land: the **number of thy days I will fulfil**.*

When you serve God he will bless your bread and water, which means that you shall not lack anything in the cost of pursuing you dreams. He will take sickness away from you so that you can stay healthy and vibrant. He will make sure that you do not have premature delivery of your dreams, you shall not experience setbacks and fruitfulness will become your portion. He even guarantees that you shall live to fulfill your destiny in a grand style. I have not seen any corporation on the earth that offers such a package, and if you know of any please don't hesitate to write me to prove me wrong. God has the best insurance policy according to the above scripture, and if you engage in serving him you are guaranteed to succeed.

If they obey and serve him, they shall spend their days in prosperity, and their years in pleasures.
JOB 36:11

If you serve God, he will ensure that you prosper in all that you set your hand to do. Many people think that serving God is a waste of time, and so they go about their normal business of pursuing their dreams and their gifts. But if you decide to serve God while pursuing your dreams, he will bless you and show you what to do to succeed in your endeavors. You should never be too busy to serve God. If he decides to take your life or allow your enemies to destroy you, that thing you are pursuing now will not succeed. You are never too rich, beautiful or successful to serve God.

Kingdom service means serving God with your time, energy, intellect and resources. Use all you have to promote the kingdom of God on the earth and you will see him promote your career, business and academics. There is nothing that you do for God or in his name that goes unrewarded. Therefore, engage in kingdom service and see your destiny glow as you become ten times better than your peers.

CHAPTER 28

Avoid Bitterness

On your way to success people will always hurt you, step on you and make you feel bad, but there is one thing you must not do, and that is be bitter. Bitterness is the roadblock to our success. Sometime your ways are going smoothly and everything is working fine; the enemy does not have any channel to hinder your progress, but then he creeps in through bitterness. Whatever anyone has done to you in the past or present, you must forgive. I know it's hard, because I was in those shoes, but you must forgive if you want to succeed. When you are bitter against someone you have built a prison about yourself, and you cannot be in prison and be free to carry out your task. Many times it is the enemy that caused those people to offend you just to force you to be bitter, in order to oppress you and hinder your success.

When you forgive people you have opened the door and allowed sunshine into your life. You have succeeded in telling the enemy of your destiny that you will not fall a victim to his ploys. Jesus said if we want God to forgive us, we must forgive others.

> *For if ye forgive men their trespasses,*
> *your heavenly Father will also forgive you.*
> MATTHEW 6:14

You cannot be bitter and pray to God to forgive your sin when you have not forgiven others for what they did to you. Sometimes what others did to you is not as grievous as what you did against God. The scripture says you should not allow the sun to go down with anger in your heart.

> *Be ye angry, and sin not: let not the*
> *sun go down upon your wrath.*
> EPHESIANS 4:26

Yes, what they did to you is inexcusable, but let it go. You deserve to be angry, but don't dwell on the anger and sleep on it. Gradually it will turn into bitterness, and bitterness is a strong spiritual blockade that will hinder your growth, progress and success. If anyone has offended you, look for that person and apologize. If you cannot see that individual give him a call, and after you have done that you will experience peace. Many times people offend you without even knowing that they have offended you; if you become bitter it makes you look foolish, because that individual doesn't even know that they hurt you. Learn to forgive, give no place to the enemy of your destiny to have a foothold. Learn to love everyone. Practice the art of advance forgiveness, that no matter what anybody does to you they are already forgiven. Don't expect the best from anybody; understand that human beings are prone to mistakes and inasmuch as we ourselves are not perfect, no one else is. As long as we are in this world, offenses will come; we must learn to look beyond the offenses of others and place our focus on what is ahead of us. That light that was once a glimpse will soon shine around us in such great intensity that others will be attracted to it.

CHAPTER 29

BE BOLD

Boldness is a prerequisite if we are to succeed and be ten times better than our peers. Fear has crippled a lot of people with great gifts, and most of the time it is fear of failure. Some people have discovered their gift and talent and have made great plans. Everything seems fine except that they refuse to take steps to actualize because of fear. You need to be bold in order to deliver your divine plan on the earth. The book of Joshua clearly shows us that God wants us to be bold.

> *Be strong and of a good courage...*
> *Only be thou strong and very courageous...*
> *Have I not commanded thee? Be strong and of a good courage; be not afraid, neither be thou dismayed: for the Lord thy God is with thee whithersoever thou goest.*
> JOSHUA 1:6, 7, AND 9

Courage is necessary in the actualization of our purpose on the earth. If you want to succeed in your gifting, you must be bold. God says you must be strong in order to succeed. You don't have to fear anything; know that God is with you. He who gave you the gift is able to help you succeed in it no matter how many people are doing the same thing. Don't allow fear to stop you from doing what God has placed in your heart to do. There is something mysterious about fear. When you despise it and make a move, you see that fear running away. I am a very shy person. Whenever I have to face the crowd to say something I literally feel I am going to fall down and die because of fear, but when I climb the podium and start speaking, in a few minutes that fear that almost killed me disappears. This means that fear is a spirit, and it can be cast out by simply taking a step. Remember, if you don't do it, no one will. Overcome your fear and you will overcome in life. God knew that Joshua might allow fear to overcome him, so he had to warn him ahead of time to be bold. Many people have allowed fear to build a prison around them; that is why they have not been able to achieve a level of success. For you to move to that next level you so desire, you must summon courage and take a step of faith. Faith is the opposite of fear, and fear is the greatest enemy of success. You hear some people say, "Take a bold step of faith," because it takes boldness to have faith. When you decide to do something and you move without looking at the circumstance around, you have clearly demonstrated faith. And when you have faith, God will be committed to making you succeed.

    I went to make a presentation one day in a very big establishment. The chairman of the company was rumored to be one of the richest men in the country, and it was to be the biggest moment in my career. During the presentation my voice was weak and incoherent, which completely showed that I was afraid. After the presentation, the chairman said to me that he liked my brand and the product but that I was not bold enough to handle the project. He then went on to say, "If you want to succeed and be great, you must be bold." I lost that project, although not the relationship with the firm, but I learned a lesson in courage. You see, some of us may have great talent and projects that may land us at the top—but because of fear we keep struggling at the foot of the ladder. Men who have succeeded in their given fields are men of courage not because they are better than you, but because they have learned to overcome their fear, and so success welcomed them. If you want to be ten times better than your peers, you must overcome that fear or else it will keep you in that valley while others are at the mountain top.

CHAPTER 30

PRAYER: THE KEY

In everything by prayer. Prayer is all that we need to succeed in life. I call prayer the foundation for successful living on the earth. It is prayer that can start everything, and it is prayer that can end it. Without prayer we certainly cannot achieve anything in life. Jesus, our model for successful living, started his earthly ministry by prayer, and when he hung on the cross he ended it with prayer. No matter your gifting, without prayer it remains dormant and ineffective. If you don't pray, life will press on you.

> *Be careful for nothing; but in every thing by prayer and supplication with thanksgiving let your requests be made known unto God.*
> PHILIPPIANS 4:6

Prayer is a requirement if we are to climb the ladder of success. The Bible says in everything we should pray; this means that nothing is too small to be taken to the altar of prayer. Don't say, "Mine are small dreams so I don't need to bother myself to pray." If you don't pray, even that seemingly small dream will never see the light of the day. During every moment in the life of a child of God the devil fights to hinder and to make sure that the plan of God for that believer will not come to pass; the only way to keep him at bay is by prayer.

Also, it is very interesting to know that prayer is the master key to unlocking all doors, and the door of success is one of them. Without prayer you will be prey in the hands of your haters and enemies who have vowed to stop you by all means. In the scriptures we see Jesus' emphasis on the need for prayer; he made us to understand that it is what we must do.

And when thou prayest....
But thou, when thou prayest...
But when ye pray....
MATTHEW 6:5-7

Jesus did not say "if" you pray, else we would say that prayer is optional. But he said "when" you pray, so that we know it is what we must do. Although prayer is essential and is a life wire of the believer, many people have been engaging in it wrongly. Not many people know how to pray, but there are guidelines to effective prayer. To start with, we must understand that prayer is a communication between two individuals and, in this case, God. Since prayer involves two people, there must be an exchange of information between the two in the course of prayer. You cannot say you are praying to God when it is only you who is talking. When you have finished you leave, but what you have succeeded in doing is a waste of precious time on the altar of prayer. That is why it is needful for you to listen while you pray. You must direct your prayer in a precise and concise manner and not with much shouting and vain repetition.

If you want to succeed in life, the best prayer you can pray is a prayer of inquiry. If you have not discovered your gift, that is what God has deposited into you to trade with on the earth. You need to pray a prayer of inquiry asking God what his purpose is for your life; ask him to show you what you were born to do, and he will show you. And if you have discovered your gift, you cannot begin to do anything without first asking him how you are to go about it. Prayer of inquiry helps us to seek direction from the throne of grace, because without God showing you what to do you may carry a great dream in your hand and fall into a ditch. When you pray the prayer of inquiry, you are telling God that you have no might of your own, therefore you want him to show you what to do.

*He shall call upon me, and I will answer him:
I will be with him in trouble; I will
deliver him, and honour him.*
PSALM 91:15

*Then shall ye call upon me, and ye shall go and
pray unto me, and I will hearken unto you.*
JEREMIAH 29:12

*Call unto me, and I will answer
thee, and show thee great and mighty
things, which thou knowest not.*
JEREMIAH 33:3

God is committed to answering our prayers and even more committed to showing us what to do if we ask him in prayer. All that God wants us to do is to call to him in prayer. He wants us to inquire from him so that he can show us what to do. God is always happy to see us come to him in prayer. There was a man in the Bible who knew how to inquire, and God was so pleased with him that he called him a man after his own heart. That man was King David, one of our favorite heroes in the Bible. David was successful because he always inquired of God what to do, and we read that he never lost any battle in his lifetime.

> *And David enquired at the Lord, saying, Shall I pursue after this troop? shall I overtake them? And he answered him, Pursue: for thou shall surely overtake them, and without fail recover all.*
> 1 SAMUEL 30:8

Prayer of inquiry is the most precise prayer we can pray. David did not ask God to come down and help him in the situation in which he found himself; instead he inquired from God if he should pursue the enemy. The response he got was a direct "pursue." God is all knowing, and if you inquire of him what to do concerning your business, career, academics and even family life, he will show you what to do to succeed and become ten times better than your peers.

EPILOGUE

So far we have learned the simple principles for outstanding success, principles that will make you become ten times better than your peers. You may see these principles as common or simple, but if you follow them you will definitely outshine all your contemporaries. I know it has been a wonderful journey, and I want to congratulate you, because we will surely meet at the top. The Bible in the book of Job 32:8 says,

> *But there is a spirit in man: and the inspiration of the Almighty giveth them understanding.*

Man is a spirit; he has a soul and lives in a body. As a born again Christian, your spirit is brand new and sinless; that is why the Holy Spirit lives inside your spirit. This new spirit enables you to hear from God, who speaks to your spirit through the Holy Spirit. And when you hear from God, he can lead you to outstanding success. Your spirit will always tell you what to do; that is why you need to listen to him. To remain a sinner is dangerous, because you are cut off from God because of the sin of Adam. It doesn't matter whether you were born in the church or if you have never committed any sin. As a sinner, you are an enemy of God, but the good news is that God's loving arms are always open to welcome everyone who comes to him through his only son Jesus, for he is the only way to the father.

> *Jesus saith unto him, I am the way, the truth, and the life: no man cometh unto the Father, but by me.*
> JOHN 14:6

Jesus is the only way to God the father, and until you accept Jesus you cannot have access to God. And when you accept Jesus, you will become a new creature; old things will pass away and everything about you will become new (2 Corinthians 5:17).

If you want to surrender your life to Jesus and be born into the family of God, please pray this prayer after me. *Lord Jesus, I come to you. I know I am a sinner, and I believe you came and died for me that I might be saved. I accept you, Jesus, as my Lord and Savior. Thank you, Jesus, for forgiving me. Thank you for saving me. Now I know my sins are forgiven. I am saved. I am born again. I am a child of God. Old things are passed away and behold, all things are become new. In Jesus name, Amen.*

Congratulations, you are now born again. You are now a member of God's family, and success runs in the family. In this family, everyone is destined for the top. God is now committed to your affairs. I made the same decision years ago, and I have no regrets. Now that you are a child of God, you will experience the love of God in your life and the riches of his glory toward you. You will, by his help, become ten times better than your peers. GOD BLESS YOU!

Note from the Publisher

Are you a first time author?

Not sure how to proceed to get your book published?
Want to keep all your rights and all your royalties?
Want it to look as good as a Top 10 publisher?
Need help with editing, layout, cover design?
Want it out there selling in 90 days or less?

Visit our website for some exciting new options!

www.chalfant-eckert-publishing.com

If you have been blessed, impacted or given your life to Jesus through reading this book, please let me know through the following means:

victoransor@gmail.com
Twitter: @victoransor
Facebook: Victor Ansor

God Bless You.

www.ingramcontent.com/pod-product-compliance
Lightning Source LLC
Chambersburg PA
CBHW022216090526
44584CB00012BB/757